This Ain't The Great Gatsby.

(Another collection of wee stories)

Walter Scott

Walter Scott © 2023

ALL RIGHTS ARE RESERVED.

No permission is given for any part of this book to be reproduced, transmitted in any form, electronic or mechanical, stored in a retrieval system, photocopied, recorded, scanned, or otherwise. Any of these actions require the proper written permission of the author.

ISBN

ScottSpace, Independent Publishing

For Correspondence Contact

walterscottpwc@gmail.com

Twitter: @WaltScott1

Contents

Introduction	v
1. Who's there?	1
2. Designer Dafty	5
3. Living the Dream	11
4. The mysterious tale of the six-inch nail	19
5. The Origin of Cryptocurrency	35
6. Trump moves to Partick	43
7. Munchies Takeaway.	55
8. PULSE N.D.E	61
9. To Insanity and Beyond	73
10. A Novella?	89
11. Christmas Spirit	97
About the Author	103

Introduction

Ding ding, seconds out, round two. Here we go again. If you liked my first book of shorts, then chances are, you'll like this one.

In book one, 'Proceed with Caution,' the underlying theme was 'substance misuse' and the darkness associated with that lifestyle, all with a humorous twist. (I put it together while at college learning about addiction counselling).

This second collection of short stories keeps that theme for three of the tales here. Of the other stories within, I touch on the subject of dementia. Two of the stories deal with minds of delusion. There's the second part of 'young Rab' and his adventures. A near-death experience and a couple of light-hearted stories complete the set. The title is a solid hint to what's not inside. These stories are unfiltered, unedited, and raw, served as they come.

All the characters are purely fictional, and any recognition is coincidental.

Who's there?

I hear the front door get battered as if it were the police.

'Hold on, hold on,' I'm shouting as I come down the stairs and have a wee peep through the spy hole.

There stands an elderly gentleman, very smartly dressed with the addition of a trilby, yip, very smart indeed.

'Who's there,' I shout as I watch him through the spyhole. He stands there with no reply.

'Who's there,' I shout again and continue to watch him. Nothing, no reply; he just stands there.

Opening the door, I nod to my mysterious visitor. 'Can I help you?'

Taking a minute, he studies me and says, 'I know you, don't I?'

'You don't know me, my friend. I'm sure I would recognise you if we had met before.'

We stand and look at each other in silence; all the time, I'm wondering who this could be.

'Listen, mate. I don't know who you are. Is there something I can help you with?'

This finely dressed elderly man stands looking at me, then asks, 'Do you know where Cauldstream Crescent is?'

I give him directions and wish him well. I don't ask any more questions as it feels a bit odd, as if the elderly gentleman isn't at his best. Something doesn't feel quite right. Closing the door, I watch from the window as he leaves.

He doesn't leave. He walks around into my back garden.

Opening the door again, I call on him. 'Hey, excuse me, what you up to? That's not the way to Cauldstream Crescent.' I give him the directions again and help him on his way. A very well-spoken and polite man he is. He thanks me and heads out of the garden this time.

My work here is done, and closing the door, I return to what I was doing before this interruption.

A few minutes pass by, and my phone begins ringing.

'Is that you W, it's Robert from round the corner. My wife's in the house, and she's freaking out. A guy is trying to get into our home, and he's at the back door. Gonna nip around and sort it out.'

'No problem, I'm on my way.' I tell Robert as I pull my shoes on and jump around.

As I'm making my way to Robert's house, something is telling me it will be that old guy trying the door. I quickly think of a wee plan if it's him. I sense that he wasn't too focused on what was happening around him.

Turning the corner, sure as, it's him. He comes

walking out of the garden and straight toward me. As he nears, I ask,

'What's your home telephone number?'

Without any hesitation or any time to think, he blurts out his home number.

The plan had been to catch him off guard with the question in the hope he'd revert to some automatic response without having time to think. (I'm hearing you think that's not much of a plan! It worked).

I phoned the number he had given me, and It's answered immediately. 'Yes. Hello, who's this?'

'Have you lost anyone?' I ask.

'Oh, please tell me you've found Bob. I've been worried sick. Please tell me you've found him.'

'Well, if Bob is a very sharply dressed man with a trilby, then I've found Bob.'

'Nice to meet you, Bob,' offering Bob my hand, we shake.

The woman on the other end of the phone is crying. I give her a minute to compose herself, then ask what area she lives in and where we should meet.

'Yes, I'll bring Bob.'

As Bob and I walk to the meeting point, we start chatting. Bob seems to have come around a bit. His focus is on its way back, and we talk about what's happened. He explains he's got dementia and how this is relatively new in his life. He's struggling to understand it all and tells me that walking has always been a favourite pastime, getting ready and striding out for a few hours in the countryside, breathing the lovely fresh air into his lungs. Now, though, Bob tells me, he just has to turn a corner, and all is lost; the world changes, and he's no idea what's happening.

I feel for him and don't know what to say. I think how horrible that must be—what an awful disease. At this time, Bob was my first ever encounter with dementia, and I didn't know much about it.

Bob's wife pulls up in her car as we arrive at the meeting place. She's very emotional and hugs Bob. 'I've told you, Bob, you can't wander around anymore. We're going to lose you for good one of these days.'

She thanks me as Bob gets into the car, and the happy couple heads home.

One of my friends now has dementia, and in his prime, he was the most articulate man I've ever met. Well educated and well-spoken. It's possible to have a wonderful conversation with him on a good day. On not such a good day, well, things can be a bit foggy.

A recently shared moment reminded me of how horrible a disease this is. We were chatting away when upon mentioning another friend of ours who had passed away a few months back. (We had attended his funeral together). My friend starts to cry. 'What do you mean he's dead? When did this happen?' His eyes flooded with tears.

What an awful disease.

I look over at my friend and wonder what he remembers of his life today.

I look over at my friend and wonder what's happening in his head.

I look over at my friend and wonder, 'Who's there?'

Designer Dafty

I'm sitting and having a coffee with a friend. She is mad about designer clothes, and everything on her has a name or label of some designer outfit. Why don't you smarten yourself up a bit, the cheeky bastard says. Now, me, I've never cared much for what I wear. If it's clean and looks OK, then I'll wear it. I don't care much if it's plain and doesn't have a trendy label, trying to make me think this piece of clothing makes me a better person or something. I just don't get it.

Why I let her comment get to me, I don't know. Anyways, her comment has got me thinking that the next time we meet, I will wear something with a designer label. I'll show her who's trendy.

I get myself organised for a shopping day that coming weekend, deciding to give up my Saturday and go shuffling around shops in town, trying to find something with a label that might make me look trendy in my friend's eyes the next time we meet.

Saturday arrives, and I head off to town, getting the

train there to save any issues with parking, and plan to persevere with the shopping until I've bought myself two items with labels. I'm not too fond of shopping, and that's me being polite about it. I find it an absolute chore and have never understood the delight some people experience with it. That's OK; each to their own, I guess.

I am trying to remain calm and patient as I enter my first trendy shop with all sorts of expensive designer stuff. That's what it is to me, stuff. I take a few steps into the store, and I'm hijacked by a sales assistant with bright red hair and a purple stripe running through it. Fair play, mate, if that works for you. His trousers are ripped at the knees, and his top looks like something I threw out years ago. (Vintage, I was later informed, is what it's now known as). He has a T-shirt in his hands, holding the top part and pulling the bottom part in slightly; he tells me this would be a perfect fit for me.

Luckily, he can't read my mind as I'm thinking, how the fuck do you know what would be perfect for me. How the fuck do you even know what I like. You've never met me and know fuck all about me. The shop is too warm, and I start to feel uncomfortable. You're all right, mate, I say to him; I want to have a wee look around. I'm not sure what I'm looking for today.

This doesn't deter his determination to act like he's my personal dresser, and he insists I follow him to view the new stock that has arrived. He says there's a discount available once I register for a store card. I don't know why I feel so hurried and harassed; maybe this is how shopping is meant to be.

I leave the store.

Finding a comfortable seat in a nearby café, I order a coffee and sandwich, deciding to rest and compose myself. That little shopping experience confirms I'm not going into any more of those trendy establishments. I am determined to buy a couple of items, so a new strategy is devised. Deciding my next shop will be a sports shop. I'll buy a pair of trendy trainers (I've no idea what's trendy) and a fancy T-shirt, hopefully, both items from the same shop to lessen the pain of visiting any more shops than required. Finishing my coffee and sandwich, I ready myself and make my way to the next sports shop along the way.

As I enter and start to look around, I feel far more relaxed here.

The sales assistants aren't harassing me; they are standing around, making themselves available to help or answer any questions if required. This is better as no one is forcing me to try things on. I'm wandering around peacefully, looking for something to catch my eye.

As mentioned earlier, I'm no wearer of trendy clothing—having no idea what brands mean or what one should wear. I decided on a pair of trainers called 'NB,' which I later learned means New Balance. I also picked a bright yellow T-shirt with the 'M' logo, which I think means Malibu, as it came from a rack beside a beautiful backdrop of Malibu, California. Obviously, I haven't gone mental and paid the ridiculous prices the first shop was charging, but having splashed out a fair bit; for me, anyway, it's splashing out. Wait til my trendy friend sees my new 'NB' trainers and yellow, stylish designer 'M' T-shirt. Bring it on. I am happy with my purchases and making my way home, thinking that perhaps shopping isn't as painful as I once imagined.

It's that time of the week when I meet my trendy designer clothes-wearing friend for a coffee and a catch-up. Wait til she sees me.

The usual time is one o'clock. There she is seated and has already bought our coffees. I hug her and take my seat. Well, check me out. Lifting my foot and showing what I think is a trendy training shoe. Telling tell her that 'NB' stands for New Balance. I put my foot back down and point at my T-shirt. Explaining to her that I'd picked this bright yellow colour by 'M' (Malibu) as I wanted to express myself more through what I wore. She sits and looks at me with a feeling sorry for me kind of stare; a minute or two passes, and nothing is said. I wonder if I've taken her by surprise with the boldness of my colour choice, and perhaps she needs a moment.

'I think you should take me with you next time you go shopping.' Then leaning forward, she peels the 'M' from the left side of my chest, 'medium,' she says, not Malibu.

Now let's get into some serious substance misuse.

LIVING THE DREAM
(MAD ALDO)

'Is that you, Annie? It's Davina here. I'm gonna need tae come doon and stay for a couple of nights as this bastard is driving me mental.'

Davina has phoned her sister in a bit of a panic.

Davina's husband, Aldo, has been on a downward spiral for some time, and his behaviour has recently taken a darker twist.

His behaviour is now completely out of control, and he can't stop drinking. The last few weeks have been hell on earth, and Davina has decided that drastic action needs to be taken. When he eventually makes it home, this time, she plans to lock him in the house. Part 2 of the plan is to remove all his clothing and shoes, thus preventing him from leaving. Part 3 of the plan is to feed him healthy food while he is locked in and try to convince him he's killing himself and it's time to get help. It's all she can think of as she's tried everything else.

'Aye, nae bother Davina. You know you're welcome here anytime,' replies her sister Annie.

'Once this drunk bastard comes hame tonight, I plan tae lock him in and hide aw his clathes. Is it aw right tae bring them doon in the motor wi me?' Davina asks.

'Aye, nae bother hen, you bring doon whatever ye want and dae whatever ye think is right.'

Davina's husband, Aldo, eventually arrives home smashed out of his mind. He's mumbling some shite about being tired and slumps onto the couch. Within seconds he is out cold, and Davina begins putting her plan into action. She knows Aldo is in a drunk coma and fuck all will disturb him, so she doesn't have to worry about him awakening as she strips off his clothing. Earlier, she had already put his other clothes an shoes in bags and into the boot of the motor. This is all part of the plan. Strip him naked and put a blanket over him. The note written earlier explaining what was happening is on the table next to him. Davina double-checks all the windows are locked. She checks the back door is locked and locks the front door as she leaves.

Game on.

Davina arrives safely at her sister Annie's house, where she plans to have a relaxing evening. She will wait until Aldo phones her tomorrow and continue with the next part of the plan.

The following morning at the other end of town...

Davie and Brian are on their way to work, feeling rather delicate from a wild weekend. It's 7.45 on a Monday morning, and both need some fizzy pop. A large can of Irn Bru is required.

Brian sees the shops up ahead and says to Davie, 'Pull in here til I get a couple of cans of juice.'

As Davie pulls into park, they both notice a strange-looking woman walking toward the van. When I say strange, what I mean is, at first glance, she seems overdressed for this time on a Monday morning. The woman wears a long, bright red party dress with purple high heels. Her hair is all over the place, and she has stubble? The lipstick she wears matches the dress but seems too thick and smudged.

'What the fuck is this coming towards us,' says Brian to Davie as they exit the van and make for the shop.

'Hey, boys, daes a favour and help me oot eh! I'm fuckin desperate here, any chance a sorting me oot wi a few quid fur a bevvy.'

Brian and Davie are momentarily stunned as they are confronted with this request in a deep voice from a woman with stubble.

'What?' says Davie as his eyes try to adjust to this unusual sight standing before him.

'Help us oot boys. I'm fuckin dyin here. I need a drink.'

Davie has a closer look and can't believe what he is seeing as it won't correlate with what his brain is telling him. As the mist in his head starts to clear a little, and things come into focus, he looks at the woman and says. 'Fuck sake Aldo, is that you?'

'Aye, it's fuckin me. Who the fuck did ye think it

wiz? You gonna geez some money fur a bevvy. I need a fuckin drink.'

'Fuckin calm doon maman. I'll gie ye some money fur a bevvy Aldo. I know masel whit it's like to be caught oot wi nae money when yer desperate fur a drink. But fur fuck sake, whit's wi the dress an heels?' says Davie.

'I've been oan a bit of a bender wi the drink, and things have gotten out of control.'

'No fuckin shit, things have gotten out of control. What's wi the fuckin rig out?' replies Davie.

'Listen, boys,' says Aldo. 'I know this looks a bit fuckin mental, but she had locked me in the hoose and removed aw ma clothes an shoes. I hud tae break oot ma ain hoose. There was fuck all for me tae wear when I came too; she hud stripped me naked an fucked off. I decided my only course of action was to pit oan her clothes and make my way up here, hoping tae bump intae some good Samaritans like yersel.'

Davie and Brian can't believe what they've encountered on their way to work this quiet Monday morning.

Davie and Brian are pissing themselves with laughter.

'C'mon tae fuck boys, geeza break here,' asks Aldo.

Davie reaches into his pocket and takes out his wallet. He peels out two twenties and hands the money to Aldo. 'Here you go, maman. I don't like tae see anyone suffering. Is that enough to tide ye over?'

'Fuckin marvellous,' says Aldo. 'That will do nicely. Cheers, man, yer a lifesaver.'

'Listen, Aldo. I need tae ask ye wan mer thing. What the fucks the lipstick aboot?'

Without any hesitation, Aldo gives what he thinks is

a genuine and honest answer. He says, 'I didnae want anybody tae recognise me.'

Well, this is way too much for Davie and Brian to handle, and they have folded with laughter.

'Fuck you,' shouts Aldo as he wiggles toward the shop to get his bevvy.

As he enters the shop, Ali, the shopkeeper, recognises him immediately and gives a wolf whistle. 'Alright, ya sexy bastard, you going on a date?'

'Don't start yer fuckin pish Ali; I'm a desperate man here. A forty-ouncer is needed pronto.'

Ali knows the score and ushers Aldo into the back shop out of the way.

'Sit there the noo Aldo til I deal wi some stuff, and I'll be in and help ye oot.'

Ali serves Davie an Brian their cans of juice while all three try no tae laugh. He then re-enters the back shop.

'Right, Aldo, whit's the fuckin score man?'

'Ali, a don't want tae talk aboot it. I just need some bevy an all be oan ma way.'

'OK, nae bother. Tell me what ye need, and I'll get it intae a bag fur ye. Is there anything a can dae tae help ye, Aldo? A mean fur fuck sake, things don't look too good here, man.'

'Listen, Ali. I appreciate yer concern, but I need some drink. Huv ye seen Maca, ma drinking buddy. Hus he been aboot? Asks Aldo.

'Aye. I saw Maca last night. He wiz in fur a carry-oot late oan. He's still up the woods living in that fuckin tent. Is that where yer heading?'

'I'm gonna head up there an join him. Chances are he'll huv a wee fire goin.'

Ali puts the booze into a bag and doubles the bag so it won't break. He hands it to Aldo and watches him leave the shop and head toward the local woods to catch up with his drinkin buddy. Ali pauses for a second and thinks, 'Aldo quite suits that dress,' then shakes his head and laughs. He thanks the gods; it's not him that's started the week with a pair of high heels oan.

Luckily, the woods are only five minutes away, and Aldo will be camouflaged amongst the trees in no time.

'Hey Maca, you there, maman?' shouts Aldo as he approaches the area where his mate has the tent pitched. Aldo can see the fire is lit and feels thankful he's made it to a safe drinking space with his pal.

'Is that you, Aldo? Aye, all is well maman. It's good, tae... Hey, you. What the fuck is this? What the fuck? Don't you try any funny business wi me, ya bastard? I'm no like that,' shouts Maca.

'Shut the fuck up, Maca, an sit doon. I'll explain everything tae ye. It's no whit ye think. Let me get a few swigs oot this boatil, an I'll set ye straight.'

'Set me fuckin straight. A um fuckin straight an a don't need any settin oot straight. Ye never telt me ye wer a wummin. What the fuck?'

Aldo takes a couple of swigs oot the boatil an passes it tae Maca. The next ten minutes are taken with Aldo explaining his case tae Maca about being locked in the hoose an huvin to break oot and then beg fur money. Maca is surprisingly attentive to Aldo's story as he's in a semi-state of shock seeing his pal dressed as a woman. Aldo finishes his tale and awaits Maca's response.

'Fair enough, Aldo, desperate circumstances require desperate measures. But I need tae ask ye one thing. What's wi the fuckin lipstick?'

'Listen Maca; yer no the first person tae ask me that an I'll gie you the same answer I gied them. It's so naebody wid recognise me.'

Maca sits looking at Aldo for a few minutes without saying a word. He takes a swig oot his boatil and continues his observations.

'Mate, we canny huv ye sittin in the wids wi they high heels oan, they must be killin yer feet. I've goat a spare pair o trainers in the tent ye can use the noo.'

'Aw Maca yer a fuckin gentleman. I've been dyin tae get these heels aff.'

Laughter erupts from Aldo and Maca at the predicament in which they find themselves.

The fire is burning well, and there is plenty of bevvy. Along with the spirits that Aldo brought, there were cans of super. Macca is also well stocked up from his visit to the shop late last night. Both men settle down to enjoy a session.

Living the dream.

I'd get comfy before reading this next one.

The mysterious tale of the six-inch nail

The following story will delve into the dark world of substance misuse.

We are about to catch up with Kevin, who is destroying his life and marriage.

Kevin is in the pub. He's been here every day for four days. His mate's gaff is where Kevin has been crashing. His mate's gaff is party central, and drugs are always around. Kevin hasn't eaten much for the last few days; he can't remember eating anything; apart from E's; he's been swallowing pills like they're going out of fashion and snorting copious amounts of 'coke.' Four days of this behaviour is hardcore, even for someone who still believes they've got what it takes to participate in this kind of madness.

It's getting on in the evening, and Kevin is halfway to being fucked out of his barnet. He's with the same wee group that has joined this monumental binge from day one. The drink is flowing, drugs are being snorted, and pills popped. Kevin likes this boozers as it's always lively and has a good sound system. There is also a small dance area.

He's been recharging his phone at his mate's gaff because of the need to replenish the drug supply, as Kevin has the connections. This need for a phone has brought its own set of problems as his wife has been trying to get hold of him and find out what is happening. Kevin's marriage has been in freefall for some time now, and this behaviour has been a recurring nightmare for his wife, who is at the end of her patience. She has had enough and wants to tell Kevin it's over, and she is packing her stuff and leaving.

He's too smashed to pay attention to the messages she's been sending and keeps deleting them. Her calls haven't bothered him as he ignores them with his phone on silent. He doesn't need to answer the phone to anyone; Kevin is surrounded by the people he wants to be with, and anything Kevin needs, he organises with a wee phone call.

Deep down, Kevin knows things are fucked. He knows his behaviour is a disgrace and that this is a bad one. Kevin wonders why his wife is still with him and puts up with his shite (**If he had read any of those**

texts she's been sending, he would know things have changed).

The music is blasting, and the group is having a ball. Some are up dancing as the drugs kick in, and the feeling is electric. Kev is buzzin and joins his pals on the dance floor.

Fourth night in a row, they are the last ones to leave the pub. No problem, though; it's everyone back to the gaff to continue the party. The house they have been returning to each night is a fuckin shithole. Kevin's mate is a manky bastard, which shows as his home resembles a crack den. The house is in an isolated spot, so there's no hassle with the music blaring and the disturbing behaviour. Nobody gives a fuck, though, everyone is smashed, and they have somewhere to continue the party.

The dealer Kevin uses waits for them as they arrive at the house. He had placed an order for a large delivery of drugs to be there when they returned from the pub. The drug orders have increased each night as Kevin tries to numb his pain. The first couple of nights had been fun, or what Kevin thought was fun, through his drink and drug-induced state. After the second night, Kevin was trying to blank out that he hadn't been to work or phoned in sick. He was trying to block out any thoughts of his wife and what she must be going through. Kevin knows he has problems, real fuckin deep mental health issues he has been suppressing for years. Anyway, the drugs are here; let's get in about it.

The drug delivery is laid out and checked on the kitchen table. It's all there, and Kevin decides to pop another four E's, washing down the pills with some Tequila, which arrived as part of the delivery. Kevin then takes a large line of coke. He knows it's all getting too much for him, but he doesn't want to face reality and figures he can keep going. Kevin doesn't want to return to reality; he can't face what horrors may lie ahead with a massive comedown on the horizon...

Day 5

Kevin becomes aware of himself and, keeping his eyes closed, adjusts to the noise in his head. He can still hear music playing in the distance and knows the music is coming from inside his head. Not being Kevin's first experience with a situation like this, he has a basic understanding of what to expect. This time though, there's a feeling of deep fear.

Something is giving him a sense things have gone too far. Way too far! He feels frightened, more scared than ever before.

Slowly opening his eyes and waiting until focus kicks in. The design on the ceiling gradually becomes recognisable as the one in his bedroom, the bedroom he thinks he still shares with his wife. Holy fuck, he thinks to himself, I've made it home.

Let's enter Kevin's head...

'Ok, ok, keep calm. How the fuck did I get here? What's the last thing I remember? I feel fuckin awful, something ain't right, and I don't just mean memory loss and being on a bender. Why, oh fuckin, why did I stay on it for days? I feel like death. What's happening with my heartbeat? Is that palpitations? Is it irregular beats? Am I gonna die? Maybe I want to fuckin die. What the fuck is that smell? Oh god, I'm soakin, fuck fuck fuck, I've pissed the fuckin bed.'

Kevin moves fast as he throws his head over the bed and vomits.

'I'm fuckin dying here, Jesus help me. What the fuck is happenin'?

Kevin vomits again, a long gushing vomit like a fireman's hose. It's everywhere, all over the wooden floor.

'Oh fuck, where is all that coming from? That's gonna seep through into the neighbours below. Fuckin hell. I need some help here. I'm dyin. I'm gonna fuckin die. I've gone too far. What the fuck's going on with my heart? Is it tryin to stop? Please, someone, help me.'

Kevin vomits again.

'Take some deep breaths. This is fuckin serious. What do I do here? I need some medical help. Where's ma phone? I need a fuckin ambulance. Where's my fuckin wife? I need help.'

Kevin starts to panic.

'You're gonna die if you don't get some help, compose yourself, man. What's ma next move, next move, next move, next move, fuck, the phone. Deep breaths, nice an easy.'

Kevin lifts his head and spots his clothes lying in a heap by the bedroom door.

'My phone has gotta be in my trouser pocket; please, God, please let it be there. How the fuck am I gonna get it? I'm fucked. I've no energy. I'm fuckin dying. I must get to the phone and call an ambulance.'

The panic in Kevin starts to increase as he truly believes he is now dying and must get medical help to save his life. He composes himself and decides to draw on all his reserves and get that phone.

'I need that phone. I need that fuckin phone. Two big deep breaths and go for it.'

Kevin takes two deep breaths, then attempts what he thinks is a leap from what he now believes to be his 'death bed' and makes a dash toward his pile of clothes.

It's not a successful attempt.

Kevin rolls off the bed onto the floor and lies in his vomit. The smell forces Kevin to flip onto his hands and knees, almost as if he is remote-controlled. He assumes a position similar to that of a hump-back bridge and proceeds to add more vomit to the substantial amount that must, by now, be seeping down through his neighbour's ceiling.

'I'm dyin here. I must get to that phone.'

He starts to crawl through the vomit toward his trousers. As he nears his clothes, his stomach starts to twist inside, like a tight knot of pain.

'What the fuck now.'

What the fuck now? He thinks as whatever remains inside him starts to run down his legs.

'Surely this must be death arriving.'

In the darts world, Kevin has hit Shanghai or a Grand Slam in tennis, golf, or rugby. Whatever way you want to view it. He has now pissed himself, vomited everywhere, and diarrhoea is running down his legs as he attempts to crawl toward his phone.

'I must get that phone and save my life. I don't want to die.' Panic has a good grip on him now, and he's convinced his life is draining away.

He reaches the crumpled pile of clothes and searches through the pockets of his trousers.

'Bingo'

Kevin looks at the phone, and to his relief, it has charge and signal.

'Maybe there is a God?'

He pushes 999, the only number in his head for a situation like this.

'Emergency services, which service do you require?'

'I'd like an ambulance, please. I think I'm having a heart attack, and my body is failing me. My organs are closing down. Please send help.'

'Could you give me your address, sir, and we will get help to you.'

Kevin gives his details.

'An ambulance is on its way, sir. What is your current situation? Would you please stay on the phone until the ambulance arrives?'

'I'm lying on the floor in my bedroom, surrounded by vomit. My heart is stopping and starting. I don't know how much longer I can hang on.'

Kevin's panic is reaching dizzying heights.

'Please stay on the line. The ambulance is on the way.'

Luckily for Kevin, the local hospital is only a few minutes drive away, and he's sure the sound of sirens is coming his way already.

Kevin has a moment of clarity which brings him to the immediacy of his predicament. He looks around the bedroom of his first-floor flat and thinks, 'What the fuck is happening here?' The vomit is everywhere, covering almost all of the wooden floor. He realises diarrhoea has been running down his legs as he crawled over for the phone. Panic and confusion are Kevin's two accomplices in this fuckin disaster.

'Are you there, sir?'

'Yes, I'm here. I can hear the ambulance nearby. Please hurry.'

The operator asks some questions to keep his attention and find his name.

'Ok, Kevin, it won't be long now. The ambulance crew have gained entry to your close and are on their way to your flat entrance. Is there any way you can get to the door and let them enter? Unlock the door. Are you capable of that, Kevin, or should they attempt to force entry?'

Kevin thinks about the big heavy door he had fitted last year. There had been a spate of break-ins, and his wife insisted on the best available security door with triple locks so that no one would ever be able to force their way in.

'Ah fuck. I think I can make it through to unlock the main door. Give me a minute til I get out of this bedroom.'

'No problem, sir. The ambulance crew is waiting at the main door now.'

Kevin reaches for the bedroom door handle and pulls himself to his feet. This takes him by surprise as he was sure, only a few minutes ago, that the only door he would be nearing was 'death's door.' He pulls on the handle. The door is stuck. There's no lock, and the door should open. He tugs on the door a little harder. The door is stuck fast.

'What the fuck is happening now.'

He tugs the door one more time. Nothing, it won't budge. He raises his head in anguish and is about to start screaming when, as his head lifts, he notices a big fuckin six-inch nail has been hammered through the door at an angle and straight into the frame. This door is not for fuckin opening.

'Noooooooooooooooooooooooooooo!'

'Are you there, Kevin? Are you there, sir? What's happening? The ambulance crew has reported hearing a scream.'

'I'm stuck in the bedroom as the door is jammed shut. I'm dying in here.' please get the fire brigade to break down the doors. Please hurry.

Kevin hangs up the phone, dropping it onto the wooden floor, where it lands face down in the vomit. He crumples to his knees with his head in his hands and begs God for a merciful and quick death.

The sound of more sirens snaps Kevin back to the hell of this reality he is experiencing. Hearing the loud sirens coming up the street, he decides to have a look at the mayhem unfolding. Getting on his hands and knees, he makes his way toward the bedroom window. The vomit and diarrhoea squelch between his fingers and toes as he slips and slides his way across the room. Delving deep into his reserves, Kevin summons enough energy to reach up and push the bottom part of the window up about twelve inches, enough to let in a blast of fresh air as it fights against the putrid smell forcing its way outside.

This Ain't The Great Gatsby.

Jesus Christ. There's an ambulance with its lights flashing and what he assumes to be a paramedic's car behind it, also with flashing lights. Here comes the fire engine with sirens and lights. There are two police cars parked next door where the flats end and the houses begin. What are the police doing here, and why are they at his neighbour's door? And, of course, the fuckin neighbours are out in full force. Kevin slumps against the wall as he adopts the sitting position. Maybe this is all a bad dream, and I will wake up soon.

BANG, BANG, BANG CRASH

Kevin knows the front entrance door to his flat is getting smashed in by the firefighters. He has another look around. Oh God, please, God, this cannot be happening. It's only a matter of seconds now.

'Kevin, sir. Are you there? Please stay back from the door, sir.'

BANG, BANG, BANG CRASH

Kevin sees the axe head busting through the bedroom door and a small gap opening. At this point, he half expects Jack Nicholson to pop his head through and shout, 'here's Johnny.' That's how fuckin crazy things feel in Kevin's head.

CRASH BANG

The bedroom door splits down the middle, and the first two firefighters enter the room, followed by the ambulance crew with their life-saving equipment.

Kevin is sure they all pause for a brief second to survey the fuckin carnage confronting them.

Kevin is propped against the wall and naked. He knows vomit is stuck to his face and hair. He doesn't want to think about what has been running down his legs. The floor is swimming with a mixture of disgust. Kevin takes a moment to console himself that they have seen worse, and it's all in a day's work.

Kevin has exhausted himself with his exertions and appears delirious. He's slurring his words, and his eyes are rolling in his head. Without hesitation, he's on to a stretcher, taken to the awaiting ambulance, and immediately attached to a drip. No time is wasted as the paramedics try to make sense of the severe condition of their patient. The ambulance quickly heads to the hospital.

At this point in proceedings, Kevin's bedroom is a busy wee place indeed. All the firefighters are trying to figure out why they had to crash open this bedroom door and can't fathom how a six-inch nail was hammered, from inside the room, through the door, and deep into the frame, making it impossible for anyone to enter or leave. They look around the room for signs of a toolbox or a lone hammer. It certainly doesn't look like a room where there would be a hammer; then again, what would a room look like with a hammer stashed? They make jokes about searching under the mattress for it. No one fancies this task. They've done what was needed, and it's time to return to the station.

As they leave the flat, Kevin's wife appears and says she will take it from here. She is mortified but also worried about Kevin. She had been at her sister's house not too far away. One of the neighbours had contacted her when the mayhem had started.

Kevin makes a miraculous recovery in the hospital and is released after only a few days. He leaves with his health fully restored and his pride in tatters as he returns home. The flat's been cleaned from top to bottom, and both doors replaced. It's as if it never happened. Kevin knows it happened, alright. He's decided to seek help with his behaviour, which has delighted his wife.

Over the next few months, Kevin did what was necessary to understand where his behaviour had been coming from and what self-development and self-discovery could do to help him move forward in a healthier lifestyle. Distance is put between him and the motley crew he used to run with. It's a complete lifestyle change for Kevin, and things are moving in the right direction. Gaining his wife's trust again takes a bit longer; however long it takes, he is willing to be patient.

The memory of that terrible day has become a bit blurry, and Kevin is thankful for this, although there is still one puzzling part that he cannot fathom.

On occasion, his wife will also ask him.

'Kevin, how the hell did that six-inch nail get hammered through the door and into the frame from inside that room?'

Before waking up in the bedroom that time, Kevin didn't remember much about how he got there. He's asked his old associates about it, but they don't remember either. It's been a difficult few months, and Kevin is adjusting to his healthier lifestyle. He is eating better and sleeping better. Things are on the up, and he likes his progress. He is mystified about that six-inch nail and finds himself, now and then, staring at the door frame and scratching his head in bewilderment.

Then one night, Kevin is jolted awake. He has a

weird dream or some kind of flashback to the night in question and the nail. In the dream, Kevin sees himself leaving his motley crew of fellow binge'rs and staggering toward his own home. He remembers feeling guilty and knowing that things have gotten out of control and must stop.

As he nears his home, he comes to the last house on the street, which has a garage. The next building is the one that contains his flat. This moment is where he hatches a brainwave of a plan. He somehow manages to get inside his neighbour's garage and steals a hammer and a six-inch nail. In his mind, he knows what has to be done.

In this dream, he gets to his bedroom, shuts the door, and hammers the six-inch nail through the door and into the frame. Kevin then decides the hammer must go; he mustn't have any way of continuing with the drink and drugs and must be confined to this room til he gets well. Kevin slides down the top half of the bedroom window, takes a few steps back, lunges at the window, and throws the hammer in a looping arch which carries it clean across the street and into the thick bushes of the gardens opposite. He remembers thinking he should have been at the Olympics as he closed the window and went to bed.

Holy fuck. Could this be what happened? Could this be the answer to the mystery of the six-inch nail? The police were at the neighbour's door; could they have reported a break-in? This could be it. Thank fuck, as it's been bothering me for too long. It's the middle of the night, so Kevin goes back to sleep and decides to investigate in the morning.

A few hours pass, and the alarm awakens Kevin. He has a coffee and runs what he remembers of the dream over in his head a few times. A plan of action is formed. Deciding if the dream is a flashback to that horrible day, then the direction he threw the hammer should lead him to the exact spot. Kevin dresses and heads outside. He's looking up at his window and visualising his earlier dream. According to the throw's trajectory, there can only be one place for this hammer to have landed—the big bush in his neighbour's garden across the street.

This is it. Climbing the fence into the garden with the big bush, Kevin has another look at his window, readjusts his thoughts on the trajectory of the throw, and pinpoints the landing area. He sees something shiny in the bush and forces the branches apart to see what's there...

It's an old fuckin coke can. Kevin searches everywhere under the big bush. There's nothing, no hammer. Maybe it was just a dream and not a flashback. Perhaps it was all just a bad dream?

The mysterious tale of the six-inch nail remains unsolved.

The universe knew we were coming. - F.D.

The Origin of Cryptocurrency

What will I have for lunch today? I'm thinking of a Subway; not had one of those in long enough. I pull in and park behind the local Subway Cafe. The car park has many spaces, so this might be a nice, quiet lunch. That's what I'm in the mood for, a foot-long Sub and a coffee; all the better if it's quiet as I'm not in the mood for busy. I place my order and take a seat; there are plenty of seats to choose from as it's empty.

Let's get in about it. I'm ready to enjoy my lunch, and the guy serving is kind enough to bring over my Sub. I've got my coffee, and my Sub looks good. I take a few bites, and it's lovely; washing it down with my coffee and all is well. I'm enjoying my lunch and the quietness.

I happen to glance up, and there he is, 'Crazy Dave.' Oh, Christ, I hope he hasn't seen me as I lower my head and practice my invisibility skills.

'Alright, bigchap, you having your lunch?'

We are off to a good start here as 'Crazy Dave' shows off his observational skills.

'I am indeed having my lunch, Dave. What you up to yourself?'

(Before going any further, I think a little background on 'crazy Dave' might be helpful. 'Crazy Dave,' as he is known locally, is bonkers. He suffered a head injury many years back caused by a motorbike crash. He is also partial to enjoying any mind-altering drugs he can get his hands on).

This could be interesting, I think to myself.

'Do you mind if I sit down,' he says and gets comfy beside me. 'My head is fuckin nipping. I've been tryna learn about cryptocurrency. All morning I've been reading articles and watching Youtube tutorials as I need to educate myself about these fuckin cryptocurrencies. Do you know anything about them?'

'Sorry, Dave, can't help you as I know nothing about bitcoin or crypto or whatever they're calling it. Can I ask why you're tryna educate yourself on this stuff? You entering into the investment market?' (Anything is possible with Dave).

'Na, no investment markets for me. I'm tryna find out about it, so I can get paid by crypto for any further shifts I do. Do you know why this fuckin crypto was invented?'

'I don't, Dave, but I've got a feeling you're gonna tell me.'

'Right, everybody was getting paid in Moon pounds when the mining started on the Moon. It was easy enough to get shifts, but what the fuck were you meant to do with Moon pounds when ye returned hame. Answer me that. You with me?'

Trying not to choke on my lunch as I wash it down with coffee and compose myself. I decided I might as well go 'chips all in' and ask,

'How long have you been working on the Moon, Dave?'

'Ah, Fuck, been about two years since I've been working away from home. It's all part of the 'Artemis 1' programme. I started mining on the Moon's dark side; with good behaviour and never being late, I got a promotion.'

'Congratulations, Dave, on your promotion. What were you promoted to?'

'Mars.'

'What?'

'Mars. I was promoted to mining on planet Mars.' He looks at me as if I'm well behind the times.

'Ok, Dave. Is that where you're working now, Mars?'

'Well, aye, kind of. It's back to this fuckin crypto bullshit. Don't get me wrong here. I'm no complaining about the pay; it's just that there's nae where tae change ma fuckin currency when returning hame. Not one fuckin shop will change my Mars pounds. I wiz havin enough problems wi the fuckin Moon pounds, and then, the added problems of Mars pounds. You keepin up wi me here?'

'I think so. You're having problems with currency exchange each time you get paid for mining duties abroad, sorry, on the Moon or Mars?'

'Aye, exactly. Hence my interest in crypto as that is now, how everyone who works there will be getting paid. Nae need to worry so much about currency exchange.'

'That's an interesting situation you're in, Dave.'

'Aye, well, kind of. You see, I'm on leave just now tae get this fuckin crypto sorted oot. Everyone's swapping over to this payment method, and if you've not got your account sorted, you'll no be getting paid. So, nae new account, nae pay. I'm learning fast, so I think I'll be up an running shortly; then, I can head off planet again.'

I have a closer look at 'Crazy Dave' to try and work out what the fuck is going on here. Is he at the wind-up or just fuckin mental? He's already off fuckin planet.

'I'm gonna have a few bites of my lunch Dave. You wanna share with me what it's like to work up there in the mines?'

'Ok. There's plenty of work going around as the mines are 24/7. Generally, it's hard work as we're mining precious gems, and some of the mines are for gold.

Big money is paid to those working the 'Helium 3' mines. That's the Helium with two protons an one neutron. It's worth about one point five billion per metric tonne. Ye need tae go on a few courses before you're allowed anywhere near they mines. There are also Silicon mines, which they use a lot tae make Silane rocket fuel. The Aluminium and Thorium mines pay pretty well too.

Three shifts. It's all machine work with the odd bit of labouring and general tidying up. Working conditions are good, with plenty of breaks; overall, it's a good *atmosphere*. It takes a bit of time to get used to working with Aliens, but once you get settled, you find that most of them are brand new. There are these wee square things that float around. At first, I thought they were mechanical things, sorry, not wee square things, wee cube things. Ye mind those Rubik's cube things, like them but about ten times the size. They're like supervisors just floating around, makin sure everything works like clockwork. I canny mind the name of the planet they come from. Anyways, you've also got the Greys; you know, the ones that are always getting spotted oan this planet, big heads, big eyes, thin arms an legs. Don't be fooled by their thin arms an legs; they can sure as fuck work the machinery as well as any of us earthlings.

You with me?'

I nod, and Crazy Dave continues.

'Then we've got the big blue bastards, blue Avians they're known as—big bastards aboot eight an a half feet tall. They run the place, but they're alright once you get to know them. Luckily, the mines are huge, and these big blue bastards have plenty of room to move around.

It's an interesting setup. There's lots of facilities for leisure time. All kinds of entertainment are available for when you're off shift. That's the problem, or that was the problem. You're oan the Moon spending yer Moon pounds no problem. You're oan Mars spending yer Mars pounds oan all the crazy entertainment available an then ye come hame an any money you've got left is a bastard tae get changed. Hence this new fuckin crypto nonsense.'

'You still with me?' He asks.

There's a bit of silence as I look at Dave and think, 'What the fuck did I just listen tae?' I've not chewed once; I don't think I've even blinked.

'Fuckin hell, Dave, that is one incredible tale you told

me.' Before I get a chance to say anything else, he's off again.

'You know one of the other problems that come wi working up there and aw that lack of gravity, having tae buy masel all sorts of different sets of clothing tae cope wi the change in ma height. I'm five inches taller just noo because I'm no long back. Don't get me rang. I'm no complaining as the pay is good.

He stands up from the table.

'Kin ye see the difference in ma height?'

I just nod.

He sits back down and stares at me like he's just described a fishing trip or something. I don't know. It seems so natural. What the fuck is going on here. How the fuck do you reply to a story like that. I think for a minute, then ask Dave. 'Have you been taking your medication?'

'Fuck you, he shouts right at my face. Fuck you. I'm tryna share what's been going on in my life, and that's all you've got tae say. Huv I been taking my medication? Of course, I've been taking my meds. Have I been taking my meds? How the fuck dae ye think I've been able tae focus oan they fuckin Youtube tutorials. Do you know how much fuckin concentration ye need? Fuck you, ya fuckin bam.'

Dave gets to his feet and storms away in what I can only assume is a huff.

Well, that was different. I have most of my foot-long Sub left, and my coffee is still warm enough to enjoy; I might as well finish my lunch. I take a bite and enjoy the flavour. Nice, things are quiet again as I sit and ponder the crazy tale Dave shared.

'Alright, bigyin, dae ye mind if I join ye?'

Turning around to look straight at Bible John, another local fuckin fruit loop. It's just no ma day.

'Aye, have a seat, John. I'll no be hanging aboot as I've got stuff tae dae.'

I'm already planning my escape.

John pulls out his bible and starts to go into his story of creationism and how the earth is only six thousand years old and blah blah blah. I can't hear fuck all anymore as I've switched off. I think John has stopped talkin. His lips have stopped moving, so taking my opportunity.

'Fuck you, John.'

I get up and walk away in what I assume John thinks is a huff. I head back to my car with my pickled brain cell, making a mental note never to buy a foot-long sub again.

I'm sitting in the car wondering about Crazy Dave and Bible John. Are they fuckin nuts? Am I fuckin nuts? Imagine Dave works in the mines on Mars, and it's me who doesn't know what's going on. I can't think that about Bible John, and all that creationist shite, though. I'm sure they still teach that in schools, mainly in America. How fuckin nuts is that?

Who's reality is reality?

Is perception truth?

Cue the twilight zone music.

The language you use to speak about yourself is as important as the food you eat.

Trump moves to Partick
Part A

Good morning Mr. Trump; how are we feeling today? As you know, this coming Friday is moving out day. You had known this wasn't your permanent residence from when you first arrived. No matter how much you have enjoyed being here, the time is almost upon us to organise your removal and transfer of belongings to your new home.

Trump takes a few moments to think over the situation he is now facing.

He has indeed enjoyed his time here and felt very comfortable in these surroundings. It's an enjoyable experience he doesn't want to give up. Deep down, Trump knows it's time to move forward. He has asked his security to find him somewhere to connect with the people. He knows he's a people person and wants to live amongst them, reconnect, and let the world know what a wonderfully warm and caring person he truly is. The last few months have been difficult; putting all that behind one and moving forward is the way to go.

It's now a waiting game until his security return with

the result of the task he had set them. Soon, he would know his new address.

Mr. Trump is escorted along to breakfast, where he enjoys his usual coco pops, and the rest of the day is his to wander around the gardens and relax. As the time to leave is almost upon him, all the necessary paperwork is complete. The hard work is over, and it's chill time.

Friday arrives…Leaving day.

Trump's security has arranged a nine o'clock to inform him of the result regarding the task he had set them.

Good morning Mr. Trump. Considering everything we know about you and allowing for your request about reconnecting with people, we have found you a flat in Peel St. Partick, Glasgow, Scotland. Here are the details of where you will be living.

Mmmmmmm, Partick, Glasgow, Scotland. I'm sure I have a golf course nearby and other business interests. Good choice thinks Trump as he listens to the finer details of his latest deployment.

Your security detail is available 24/7 and will escort you wherever you may decide to wander as you explore your new surroundings. We understand time will be needed for adjustments to your new environment. Your issued security has been briefed on their requirements to help make the transition as smooth an experience as possible. We have deployed two of our most experienced operatives.

I like the sound of this. Partick, Glasgow, Scotland, where I can reconnect with family, return to my roots, and learn about my ancestry. It's been too long, and the time is right to start conversing with everyone. Yip, I like this plan.

We shall arrange for the presidential car to pick you up at lunchtime and begin your move. In the meantime, could you ensure that you have everything packed and said your goodbyes?

Trump dismisses his security detail and packs his final possessions into a small carry bag as he awaits the arrival of his transport.

'Ok, Mr. Trump, it's time. Let's go.' With a security detail on either side, Mr. Trump is led out of the building and into the waiting car as the journey to Peel St., Partick, Glasgow, Scotland, begins.

What turns out to be a relatively straightforward journey nears its end as the vehicle pulls up outside Mr. Trump's new place. 'Here we are, Mr. Trump, arrived safe and sound. I hope that wasn't too long or too boring for you. We tried to make it all as smooth as possible.' One security detail collects Trump's belongings from the car boot while the other leads him toward his new dwelling.

All three enter the flat and look around, ensuring everything is in order and in place for Mr. Trump to settle in. All is well, and after showing Trump where the security detail will be living, he is left alone in his new flat.

I like this. Everything is new, and the place has a fresh coating of paint. Yip, I'm happy with the view, looking out over the cricket grounds, lovely. My security detail is nearby and easily summoned by pulling a cord, anytime, day or night. This will do me nicely. I'll relax tonight and get a good night's sleep. Tomorrow we can begin meeting my public and reconnecting with all my beautiful supporters.

Trump puts on the tv and settles for the news channel. It's all doom and gloom, more terrorist attacks, and general mayhem. He knows it's all designed to keep people living in fear. He knows most of its made-up bullshit and make-believe solely for the purpose of control. After a few hours of the fear-mongering news, he feels sleepy and heads to bed—his first night in the new flat. The bed is wonderfully comfortable, and in no time, he is in the land of nod.

A new day and a fresh start. Trump has slept well and looking forward to the day ahead. He showers and dresses, then summons his security detail to inform them he is ready for today's excursion. Trump finds it a bit strange he will only be accompanied by one of his security today and thinks that Partick must indeed be an incredibly safe place to stay.

And off out they go...

One could not have asked for a better day to meet his supporters. The sun is blazing in the sky, and there's a cricket match about to begin along the road. 'Let's head toward the cricket match and see how the crowd responds to my presence,' he tells his security guy. His escort finds this slightly odd but not enough to set any alarm bells ringing.

They head along the road and can hear the crowd's murmurings as the match is about to begin.

CRACK! The first ball strikes hard off the bat.

Trump hears the crack of the bat striking the ball and

dives for cover. In Trump's mind, this can only mean one thing. They've come for the president. Somehow they know he's in Partick and have mounted a terrorist attack. He has to survive this and decides to dash to safety. He breaks away from his security, who is taken by surprise as Trump runs for freedom toward Dumbarton Rd. He's gotten a good one hundred yards away from his escort and is moving fast (he's always kept himself fit). Without hesitation, he jumps into the presidential car, aka 'The Beast' with its 4-inch armoured plating, and takes off at high speed just as his security arrives on the scene to see him disappear into the distance...

Part B

Good morning Mr. Holland; how are we feeling today? As you know, this coming Friday is moving out day. You had known this wasn't your permanent residence from when you first arrived. No matter how much you have enjoyed being here, the time is almost upon us to organise your removal and transfer of belongings to your new home.

Mr. Holland takes a few moments to think over the situation he is now facing.

He has indeed enjoyed his time here and felt very comfortable in these surroundings. It's an enjoyable experience he doesn't want to give up. Deep down, Drew Holland knows it's time to move forward. He has asked his carers to find him somewhere he can connect with the people.

Drew feels he's a people person and wants to live amongst them, reconnect, and let the world know what a wonderfully warm and caring person he truly is. The last few months have been difficult; putting all that behind one and moving forward is the way to go. It's taken a while for the doctors at Gartnavel royal hospital to find a balance with Mr. Hollands' medication that allows him some clarity without too much drowsiness. It's been difficult for the doctors to find the right balance of medication to subdue Drew's delusions.

It's now a waiting game until his carers return and let him know the whereabouts of his sheltered housing.

Drew is escorted along to breakfast, where he enjoys his usual coco pops, and the rest of the day is his to wander around the gardens and relax. As the time to leave is almost upon him, all the necessary paperwork is complete. The hard work is over, and it's chill time.

Friday arrives...Leaving day.

Drew's team of carers has arranged a nine o'clock to inform him of the details regarding his departure.

Good morning Mr. Holland. Considering everything we know about you and allowing for your request about reconnecting with people, we have found you a flat in Peel St. Partick, as we know you have some relatives nearby who are happy for you to move there and be close to you.

Your carers are available 24/7, and of course, you will be accompanied by at least one carer wherever you decide to wander. We understand time will be needed for adjustments to your new medication. Your carers have been fully briefed on their requirements to help make the transition as smooth an experience as possible. We have given you two of our most experienced carers.

Mr. Drew Holland nods and smiles as he takes all this in.

We shall arrange transport to pick you up at lunchtime and begin your move. In the meantime, could you ensure you have everything packed and said your goodbyes?

As his carers leave, Drew packs his final possessions into a small carry bag as he awaits the arrival of his transport.

'Ok, Drew, it's time. Let's go.' With a carer on either side, Mr. Holland is led out of the building and into the waiting car. His journey to Peel St., Partick, begins.

What turns out to be a relatively straightforward journey as the hospital is just along the road nears its end as the vehicle pulls up outside Drew's new place. One carer collects Drew's belongings from the car boot while the other leads him toward his new dwelling. Here we are, Mr. Holland, arrived safe and sound.

All three enter the flat and look around, ensuring everything is in order and in place for Drew to settle in. All is well, and after showing Drew where the carers live in this sheltered housing, he is left alone in his new flat.

I like this. Everything is new, and the place has a fresh coating of paint. Yip, I'm happy with the view, looking out over the cricket grounds, lovely. My carer is nearby and easily called by pulling a cord, anytime, day or night. This will do me nicely. I'll relax tonight and get a good night's sleep. Tomorrow we can begin by going for a short walk and see how it feels to be outside again.

Drew puts on the tv and settles for the news channel. It's all doom and gloom, more terrorist attacks, and general mayhem. He knows it's all designed to keep people living in fear. He knows most of its made-up bullshit and make-believe solely for the purpose of control. After a few hours of the fear-mongering news, he feels sleepy and heads to bed—his first night in the new flat. The bed is wonderfully comfortable, and in no time at all, he is in the land of nod.

A new day and a fresh start. Drew has slept well and looking forward to the day ahead. He showers and dresses then contacts his carer to inform him he is ready for today's excursion. Drew finds it a bit strange that he will only be accompanied by one of his carers today and thinks he must be making progress.

And off out they go...

One could not have asked for a better day to be out and about. The sun is blazing in the sky, and there's a cricket match about to begin along the road. 'Let's head toward the cricket match and see how the crowd responds to my presence,' he tells his security guy. His carer finds this slightly odd but not enough to set any alarm bells ringing.

They head along the road and can hear the crowd's murmurings as the match is about to begin.

CRACK! The first ball strikes hard off the bat.

Drew hears the crack of the bat striking the ball and dives for cover. In Mr. Drew Holland's/Trump's mind, this can only mean one thing. They've come for the president. Somehow they know he's in Partick and have mounted a terrorist attack. He has to survive this and decides to dash to safety. He breaks away from his security, who is taken by surprise as Drew/Trump runs for freedom toward Dumbarton Rd. He's gotten a good one hundred yards away from his escort and is moving fast (he's always kept himself fit). Without hesitation, he jumps into the presidential car, aka 'The Beast' with its 4-inch armoured plating, and takes off at high speed just as his carer arrives on the scene to see him disappear into the distance.

Drew Holland has hijacked a car stopped at traffic lights. His delusional mind has gone wild, and, convinced he is Donald Trump, quick as a flash, he's pulled out the elderly driver, jumped into the car, and sped away as his carer arrives to see the car speeding into the distance. His carer phones the police, and a chase begins...

(The mind can be a minefield. The mind can be your best friend or worst enemy: multiple personalities, schizophrenia, and all the other mental health challenges out there. How horrible must it be to suffer from powerful delusions)

As Drew Holland speeds away in the hijacked car, believing he's Donald Trump and under attack from terrorists, his carer has alerted the police, and a short chase ensues. It's only a brief chase because Trump believes the police to be on his side and part of his security, so he pulls the car over as he feels safe.

On his return to Gartnavel hospital, Drew Holland spends a further three months undergoing treatment, tests, and therapy until, once again, the professionals decide he is fit to be released back into society. During these three months, one of his relatives passes away and, in their Will, leaves Drew H (as he likes to be known after his release from hospital) a four-bedroom flat on the outskirts of Glasgow. That's where Drew H is living when we catch up with him later...

Life is more or less a farcical outcome of a chain of accidents- S.W.

Munchies Takeaway.

Let's introduce...

Antoine Roccamora, aka ' Tony Rocky Horror.' (Sue me, Tarantino)

Tony is what he's known as to his customers. Tony runs the local takeaway shop and has done for years. It's always done good business and been popular with the local people. After a recent refurb and menu change, it's not just popular with the locals; people have been coming from far and wide to sample Tony's culinary delights.

Tony's a people person and loves the banter with the customers. He's always joking and laughing and having the crack with his regulars. This recent increase in business has made him an even happier man. Over the weekends, when the shop is at its busiest, his customers are returning for second helpings, and Tony loves it; cha-ching goes the till.

Tony's a people person, for sure. 'Munchies Takeaway' it's a happy wee place.

Tony has always done good business. He is a businessman and a people person, but a businessman first, no less. This recent refurb has cost Tony a pretty penny, and he's looking for a good return from his investment, as any businessman would. The new menu has been going down a storm, and business is booming. Not much has changed from the original menu. There have been changes, but not wholesale changes: little tweaks here and there, some name changes, and adjustments to various ingredients. Tony's sauces have always been famous. 'Do you want the red or pink sauce, or perhaps one of each?

Tony adds the wee container of sauce to each order. 'There you go, sir, enjoy your meal.' Always with a smile. Each time Tony puts one of his special sauces into an order, there's a little glint in his eye. Tony's a people person and enjoys having happy customers. It's a happy wee place.

Bringing in extra staff since the refurb has created a good balance of old hands and new trainees, making for a happy workplace. All is well in 'Munchies Takeaway.'

It was quite the refurb—a big job from top to bottom. The whole shop was stripped bare and completely redone. The place looks great, and everyone is always giving Tony compliments on how wonderful the shop looks and how incredibly tasty his food is. Tony loves it. He's always smiling and has that wee glint in his eye as he adds a tub of his famous sauce to each order.

Aye, Tony's a people person.

During the refurb, which seemed to take forever,

Tony would appear from time to time and check on how the shop was coming along. You would see him the odd time, and people would ask, 'Hey Tony, what's taking so long? We're starving to death around here,' his customers would joke with him. Tony would always reply, 'Don't worry, there's been a couple of hiccups with this or that or whatever.' There was always something holding up the progress. The local people just got used to what was happening and what will be, will be.

The builder carried out all the work using the back entrance, where no one could see. You would notice the odd lorry here or there, coming or going. But no one paid much attention. There did seem to be a lot of movement for a refurb of this size. I'm sure it will be ready when it's ready, was the consensus amongst the locals.

Anyways, time passed, and the shop opened with much appreciation. And as I said, the people love it, and it's been a booming success.

'What're the ingredients in this sauce, Tony? It's bloody lovely.'

'I canny tell ye that. It's a secret family recipe from way back.'

Aye, Tony's a people person. It's a happy wee place, 'Munchies Takeaway.'

One of the new additions to the shop was a fancy walk-in chiller. It was an expensive-looking thing and must have cost a few quid. It was always locked? From the first day of reopening til now, no one has seen this chiller open. A big fancy shiny aluminium door. Maybe it wasn't aluminium; perhaps it was some kind of alloy?

Who cares what it was made of? It was never unlocked or opened. Not that customers pay any attention to this kind of thing. They were delighted with the new menu and the incredible special sauces.

Business boomed, and everyone was happy.

Now, there was one difference since the refurb that no one knew about. That was Tony, and his right-hand man Faisal, aka 'Pretty Boy' (he is always well groomed and takes pride in his immaculate appearance), were now solely responsible for the new unique sauces. No one was allowed to be around when Tony and Faisal went to work and produced these beautiful sauces that thrilled everyone's taste buds.

When Tony and Faisal were about to do their magic and produce the sauce, they would ensure the shutters were closed and no one was around.

Then, and only then, Tony would unlock the chiller door.

This was no ordinary chiller. It may have looked like one from the outside, but that's where the resemblance ended. The chiller door opened to reveal a short set of steps leading downward toward an underground room. A modern scientific-style room with various gadgets and switches on the wall as one entered. A room with a top-of-the-range extraction system installed. This is where the magic happened, and the sauce production took place—no ordinary type of underground room but one with temperature and humidity control.

The reason for all the gadgets and top-of-the-range equipment was that this is Tony's special room. This is

Tony's grow room. This is where Tony grew strong, potent marijuana. The special ingredient in the sauce.

Aye, Tony's a people person. A happy wee place, 'Munchies Takeaway.'

'Would you like an extra sauce with that, Sir lol?' Business is good.

PULSE N.D.E
(Near-death experience)

For many years now, and many reasons, I've been curious about what happens after we die. It wasn't always like this. I remember my younger days when I believed when we're gone, we're gone, being one of those 'we return to the earth from which we came type thing, worm food, that's what we become.' My connection with the experience of death and of losing a loved one hadn't begun. My awareness of the subject was non-existent. You could say a bit of a heathen or perhaps better described as an atheist. When reflecting on those times, I remember ranting about religion, its connection with controlling the masses, and the number of deaths associated with my God's better than your God type thing. Anyway, things have significantly changed from those times, including my awareness and life experiences. Now more spiritual with belief in a universal force of sorts, but before getting any further into that, let's

detail a near-death experience a friend of mine, Danny, went through, and we'll take it from there.

-Danny-

'A few years back, I was involved in a car crash. Any car crash is bad enough, but this one, at the time, well, it could have been a lot worse. I was alright; a bit shaken but alright. It wasn't till months later it became apparent that my back wasn't functioning as it should, and I was experiencing increasingly severe pain in my lower spine. The Doctor ordered me to attend various tests, and the seriousness of the situation began to unfold.

The medics informed me that I required spinal surgery and had no other option. If we don't operate soon, you may lose the ability to walk.

It's not exactly what anyone wants to hear.

Around this time, my father passed away, and it transpired that my surgery was to take place the day after his funeral. Under different circumstances, the arrangements for surgery would have been rescheduled. It was a tough time, indeed. I knew it was serious stuff. Still, the words 'you may lose the ability to walk' reverberated around my head, and I decided to keep the arranged appointment.

Appointment day...

On the day of surgery, I arrive at the hospital feeling a little apprehensive. Saying goodbye to my father the previous day and with those words bouncing around my head, 'you may lose the ability to walk' made for a weird mixture of emotions. There was no turning back, and 'I'm here now' as they say. After settling in and going through the pre-op procedure, we all head to the theatre, and the surgeons do their thing. I vaguely recall being wheeled out of surgery and into the post-op ward, which has five other people in beds. I'm not quite lucid at the time, presumably from the drugs used to anaesthetise me for the operation. I must have fallen asleep as all I knew was I remembered nothing else until startled by a loud noise.

I quickly realised the noise source was the machine beside my bed. The alarm is sounding, and I'm aware that all the readings are blank. I remember thinking, 'what the fuck' this does not look good.

At this point, I'm not sure if I'm awake or what's happening, but I know a nurse comes running into the ward. I hear her footsteps as she approaches and checks the readings on the machine, or lack of readings is more accurate, then she runs off.

The crash team arrives, and events take an unusual twist. (As if things aren't unusual enough already).

I see the curtains getting closed around my bed. There are several medics with varying job descriptions. They all seem to know their tasks and are performing in a very proficient and professional manner. I'm watching them do their thing when I suddenly realise I'm sitting up. I don't notice my body lying flat on the bed as I'm overcome with an incredibly intense feeling that I'm no longer part of this world, this realm, where the medics are working. As the weirdness of the situation strikes me, my attention focuses on the medics who, I now realise, are trying to revive me. Time, as I once knew it, doesn't exist. I'm somewhere where linear time no longer matters. I'm fuckin dead, but I'm somehow here?

My sense of detachment increases as I now know I can control time. It felt like if I looked forward, I could move time into the future, or if I looked back the way (over my left shoulder), I could move/see time going backward. I could fast forward or rewind time as I chose.

A weird sensation indeed to add to the already increasing bewilderment.

Adjusting to my new realm of consciousness, I decide not to put my time-altering skills to the test, as, for the moment, my focus is on the fascinating subject of resuscitation and the medics attempting to bring me back to the land of the living.

I can see everything happening with my now 360-degree vision and begin noticing more details of my surroundings. There's an older nurse with dyed blond hair, her roots starting to show. She is at the top of the bed, constantly talking in my ear, 'Come on, Danny, stay with us. Come on, Danny, stay with us,' repeat, repeat, repeat. Although fully aware of my surroundings and seeing the medics trying to revive me, the older nurse speaking in my ear holds my attention. She has a tattoo on the back of her neck, a very intricate design of a butterfly with beautiful reds and greens, which bring the butterfly to life. It truly is beautiful.

This next bit, I've never told anyone till now. I don't know why; it always felt a bit out of place, considering what was happening...

At this point, whatever I am, an entity, an energy, a spirit, whatever you want to call it. I can move around, like float about; it's hard to describe and put into words. Anyway, I find myself beginning to laugh as I float around in front of the faces of the medics, and at one point, I'm waving, or what feels like waving, and saying silly things like 'you can't see me, can you?' And 'I'm here, and I'm invisible,' mental, eh!

It's now my visitors from this new otherworldly realm arrive.

The curtain is pulled open, and two small, shabbily dressed men are standing. Their sudden appearance diverts my attention from watching the nurse speak in my ear. My initial thought is, what are the orderlies doing here, then one of the men smiles at me, the one on my right, and I know, at that moment, they are here, with me, in this otherworldly realm. We look at each other for a moment, then the one who had smiled makes an inquisitive gesture and says, 'Well, are you coming?' When I say, he says to me, what I mean is that it's more an exchange of energy, a telepathic communication that feels like speech—strange stuff.

I decline his offer, and everything goes blank.

The medical team brings me back to life. My heart starts beating, and my pulse begins.

Eventually, when I came around, I was once again surrounded by the medics, all doing their thing. As they finish their checks and move away, I recognise the nurse approaching my bed. I see her dyed blond hair with roots starting to show. She leans in close to me and says, in a voice, I recognise, 'You had us worried, Danny, you really had us worried.' As she tucks in my sheet and turns away, I notice the beautiful butterfly on the back of her neck.

I look over at the other five patients in the ward, all staring at me with a mixture of trepidation, fear, and awe. And that is my story.'

'Thanks for sharing your story with me. I love these stories as I'm curious about what happens when we pass. Hearing this story first-hand adds to my curiosity. I would like to know what an experience like that would do to someone. Would you have described yourself as religious before this happened? Have you become religious since it happened? Do you think there's a God? Do you think there's an afterlife? Has it changed your behaviours in daily life?'

-Danny-

'Although I regard myself as unaffiliated to any particular religion. Before entering the operating room, I decided that I would survive this, no matter what happened, and offered a prayer. In the prayer, I asked to have no problems during the operation and would return home safely to see my children afterward. Having no idea why I did this, but it felt right.

I've always had an ill-defined sense of what God and an afterlife may be. Still, I never felt the need to explore or express it and have never been drawn to any religion, as I was raised in a secular house where my family openly mocked religion.

I've experienced other instances that I'm certain occurred to save me from imminent danger or were experienced as a reminder/guide that there is another life beyond death and something we humans call God. One example of this was as a young child; I had an accident that left me unable to move any muscles on the right side of my body for about three months. I have memories of my spirit/soul floating downstairs and hovering outside the living room door, listening to my parents talk.

My world of dreams has always created interesting connections with life, such as the ability to dream about future events in minute detail. I can also sense evil far better than before. The detailed dreaming hasn't changed since my experience; it's something I still do, although it doesn't worry me so much now as my experience, for me, was definitive confirmation of an afterlife. Confirmation I have unfinished business and will not die until this business is concluded. The only way of describing this is in supernatural terms: Of a manifestation or event attributed to some force beyond scientific understanding or the laws of nature.

During my otherworldly near-death experience after my operation, I believe the appearance of the two apparitions to be a connection with Angels, and my pre-op prayer was a connection with this happening.

I believe an afterlife exists, and this experience only confirms an already strong but ill-defined belief in God and a different form of existence from the one we perceive on earth.

The only other moderate change in my life was I deplore the irrational hatred of others even more than I did before, having even less time now for selfish people.

Life, as we know it, in this form, is too short.'

'Brilliant. You and I have similarities in our belief in an afterlife. I know your experience took place a while back, and It's left me wondering if, having had time to reflect, are you any wiser about what we may encounter in the afterlife. I believe there's definitely something awaiting us, but what that something is, I'm not sure.'

-Danny-

'I don't know what we may encounter in the afterlife, but I'm certain there is one. After being given the all-clear and getting home from the hospital, in the following weeks and months, the experience got me thinking more and more about what had taken place during my near-death experience. I began questioning it and would re-run the whole sequence repeatedly, searching for any significant meaning for me and my life. Each time I re-ran the sequence of events, I could feel and sense everything in the same way it happened. It was a strange sensation returning to this heightened state of awareness as if I were back in the moment.

I continued trying to figure out what happened and its significance for my life until I began having a recurring dream in which I was dead and travelling through the universe in a transparent tunnel. As I travelled along this tunnel, it got hotter and hotter to the point where I would awaken with the sweat lashing out of me, fearing it was the burning fires of hell. That's how hot it felt, and I've no idea why I was connecting it with the 'burning fires of hell.' This recurring dream happened for some time until, on one particular night, the journey through the transparent tunnel continued beyond the hot, burning sensation. I was launched into the light at the end of the tunnel, into what I can only describe as an incredible, magnificent, freeing place of heavenly wonders. An all-encompassing vast sea of light penetrated through my soul's essence with feelings of love, compassion, and forgiveness. I felt illuminated with profound beauty and was completely present in every moment.

All the galaxies of the universe surrounded me, and I was ecstatic, an almost indescribable place to be.

I awakened feeling incredible.

There was no more recurring dream after this.

In that final dream, I received a message. I don't know how this happened, but I received a message telling me to read the last part of the Old Testament. Once again, I had no idea why, as I don't affiliate with any particular religion, but that was the message.

So, I searched and found a bible, flicked through to the latter part of the Old Testament, and had a read. What was on those pages surprised me, and I'm still trying to work it out. What does it all mean, and how is it connected with my near-death experience and life?'

Wow, that's some story, maman, and thanks again for sharing. I love this kind of thing. And as exotic as your account is, it's pretty mild compared to some other near-death experiences where the participants are wonder-struck and come across an endless cascade of gods—African Gods, Egyptian, Greek, Hebrew, Christian, Islam, and Native American. There are instances of encounters with the great Allah shimmering with grace beyond grace.

Some of the ones I've read encounter the Buddha as a living lotus or meet Lord Krishna with glistening iridescent blue skin radiating absolute power. It's all intertwined and all valid, just different names covering an all-compassing force. I read it described as the transforming light of the Gods.

It's mental, wondering about the possibilities of what, if anything, might be next.

Who and what is not God?

What does God mean to each individual? Is the universe the body of God?

We are all connected; we are all one, a oneness interacting with a matrix of unimaginable energy. A super consciousness of a higher realm of self. Do we enter a dimension of magnificent love and energy?

What's the connection between spiritual awakening, higher levels of meditation, psychedelics, and near-death experiences?

Is it all different pathways to the same place?

To become transformed and emersed in love. To be embraced and changed in a way where you will never be the same again. After travelling through the tunnel of light and experiencing a profound oneness, connecting all souls. How can one view life in the same way after this transformation?

I understand that the journeys are custom tailored, depending on each individual's belief system. No matter what religious background or philosophical leanings one may have, everyone will experience a slightly different angle of defining

God, the universe, good and evil, love and fear. It's incredible learning about all these near-death experiences and their similarities with the various realms encountered while using psychedelic drugs. Are they connected?

There's a hypothesis that says, at the moment of death, our Pineal gland releases DMT, causing hallucinations. Some return to share their experience, and some don't. So, how do we know what happens to the ones who don't return? Apart from death, obviously.

There's no humorous twist at the end of this story. I wanted to provoke thought about the afterlife, God, hallucinogenic drugs, and in what ways, if any, they are all connected.

Perhaps it's a miracle that we are here. Each morning we awaken and each new sunrise. Who's going to be around for sunset? The universe can take you at any moment...sitting reading a book, walking to the shop, watching tv, driving home, eating dinner, enjoying your sleep...the reaper can appear any time.

Enjoy your day.

To Insanity and Beyond
(Part 2 of 'Young Rab')

Here's a little recap of part one.

Young Rab was having a disastrous run of events. In his sleep world of dreams, he's constantly battling demons and has destroyed Thoth. However, Goddess Bastet was still a problem young Rab had to deal with. These recurring dreams weren't helping his mental state. There was also the running face first into the patio doors incident, and then finally, at that party, his remaining good eye had decided to jam inwards facing his nose. He had fled the party, wondering if he had a brain tumour. That's where we left him...

Rab arrives at the hospital as his mind slowly starts to dissolve into insanity and beyond.

Straight to the reception desk walks Rab.

'Please, can someone help me? My eye is pointing inwards, and I'm worried I may have a brain tumour.'

The receptionist can see that Rab is distressed and gently takes some details from him as they wait for a doctor to become available. She is also concerned that

Rab is under the influence of something, but he's obviously in need of help.

The doctor becomes available.

'OK, Robert. Is it OK if I call you Robert?' Asks the doc.

'Sure'

'There's a definite issue with your eye. Your pupils are enormous, and I'd like to establish what's happening here. What can you tell me about this? Did you wake up like this and make your way here? I'm concerned that you may have been taking something. Are you under the influence of drink or drugs?'

As the doctor examines Rab and asks questions, he shines a small torch into his eyes as part of the examination. At this point, Rab's mind wanders to a weird place for a few seconds. He imagines being captive on an alien ship, and this is the beginning of a sequence of events ending with an Anal probing. Rab snaps out of his reverie and focuses on the situation at hand.

Rab is no stranger to finding himself in unusual situations over the past while, especially since his binge drinking and drugging have reached new heights of depravity. During this time, he has developed a refined repertoire of bullshit and an excellent set of skills in thinking on his feet for explanations and excuses.

Rab explains that at work, he'd been alongside someone using a mini-digger, and the excavation bucket had spun around and hit him in the face causing the cuts and bruising he was now displaying. Rab was happy with his level of bullshitting. He tells the doctor that earlier, with his evening meal, he'd had a couple of glasses of wine and felt unwell, so he went to bed early, hoping a good sleep would help.

The doctor was a veteran and had probably heard every line of bullshit known to humankind. He knows Rab is an absolute talker of bollocks, but he's still a patient with head injuries and something going on with his eye. Under different circumstances, the doc would have Rab removed by the police for turning up here, so fucked out his mind, but this time Rab's luck is in. The doc tells Rab he's getting kept in for observation, and they will give him a sedative and a bed for the night. In the morning, they will put Rab forward for a scan and carry out a complete set of examinations.

Rab asks if there is a chance he's got a brain tumour. The doc tells him not to worry about that and gives him the sedative. Arrangements are made, and Rab is escorted to his room for the night, where sleep awaits as the strong sedative begins to work.

Rab comes around as the morning light wakes him up.

What the fuck? A hospital, I'm in a fuckin hospital bed. Aw, Christ. What can I remember this time? Rab plays any available memory from last night.

As best he can, Rab pieces together last night's exploits and tries to work out how he ended here.

Right, fuck this, he thinks and slowly gets out of bed; he's got a drip attached and doesn't want to knock it over. It's on one of those mobile frames, so pulling it with him, he moves to the mirror in the ensuite toilet to look at his face.

Fuckin hell, man. Look at you. What are you doing to yourself? Rab thinks as he works out what to do next. Seeing his eye has reset itself, he thanks the gods for that. Next move, let's get the fuck out of here. His clothes are in the cupboard next to the bed. Rab pulls the drip from the back of his hand, tears off his paper gown, and gets dressed. He takes a piece of the paper gown with him to press onto the back of his hand to stop the bleeding that removing the drip has caused.

Rab walks straight out the front door and talks to no one as he wants to be home and feel safe.

On arriving at his house, Rab heads to his stash of Valium. He still has quite a few left and breathes a sigh of relief. His head is a bit fuzzy from the sedative at the hospital, and he wonders what to do. Do I take four or five Vallies and crash on the couch? Will I zone out and forget all my troubles for a few hours? Perhaps I should take six or seven? Will they put me into a deep sleep with no dreams? My dream world is painful with these fuckin recurring dreams of fighting demons, and I'm wondering which is worse, my dream demons or the demons that are troubling me in my everyday life.

Rab swallows eight Valium and assumes his position on the couch, pulling the duvet over and flicking the tv remote until he finds a suitable channel he can leave on for background noise. Rab gets comfy and refuses to let his mind wander, determined to let his head get some rest. The Valium slowly kicks in, and Rab drifts off.

For the first time in a long time, Rab feels quite good.

The Valium hit hard, and he sleeps right through eighteen hours. Everything happening must have caught up, and a glorious sleep was needed. It's his best sleep in a long time, and as he sips his coffee, Rab feels almost Human. What am I gonna do? He asks himself. I can't continue this reckless behaviour, ruining what's left of my life. I need a plan to stop all this bingeing with booze and coke. **(This next bit may be one of those moments that seemed like a good idea at the time, as Rab's new plan is smoking weed. That's his plan! He thinks that if he gets into smoking lots of weed, he won't have the strong urges to consume copious amounts of booze and cocaine)**. Rab phones and arranges for a large amount of weed to be dropped off and starts thinking about the upcoming weekend and how to prepare for it.

The weed arrives. Rab decides to have a few joints and a blast of a Bong he keeps under the sink. He is viewing this as a trial run, a scouting mission to discover if this plan may actually work. Could this be what's needed to numb the strong urges that envelope him and drive him toward drinking an drug binge's?

The weed is potent, and before long, Rab is comfortably numb. Having smoked three joints and had a blast of the Bong. All feels well in Rab's world, and he's confident this new plan is a winner and weed is the solution to curb the powerful urges driving him to despair.

Looking forward to the coming weekend where, for once, he is ready for combat. That's how powerful Rab's urges are; he regards his preparations as the equivalent of prepping for battle.

Rab starts to feel a bit peckish. It's more than a bit peckish; it's more like a wave of ravenous hunger hitting him like a sledgehammer, and food consumption is now of the highest order. He makes his way to the kitchen, hoping to discover what delights await in his larder...

Quickly buttering a slice of bread and taking a bite as he pops another two pieces into the toaster. Rab opens a tin of beans and empties them into a pot, taking another bite of bread as he opens a packet of blue riband biscuits and stuffs one into his mouth, washing it down with a swig of ice-cold milk. Rab is enjoying himself as everything he eats tastes marvellous. Rab knows he's stoned out of his mind and in the grip of a munchie attack. What can one do? he thinks.

'Go with it:' and slides another biscuit into his mouth.

The beans are slowly beginning to warm as the bread pops from the toaster. Rab doesn't hear the little ping noise the toaster makes when done as he is trying to chew open a packet of bacon. Things are getting out of hand as Rab can't decide what to put into his mouth next. Looking over, he spots the box of coco pops and knows adding them to the eating plan is a must.

While reaching for the coco pops, he receives a signal from his stoned mind. 'Pour the coco pops into the pot with the beans. You like both, and why have you never thought of this before?'

Rab is now fucked and completely wasted. He stuffs another two blue ribands into his mouth and swigs the milk. Realising the toast is ready, Rab applies lashings of butter. With toast in hand, he lifts the pot with the beans and coco pops mix and makes his way into the bedroom. He decides a wee lie doon will be needed after this delicious dinner.

Why have I never thought of this before? Thinks Rab as he spoons the bean/coco pop mix onto the toast and devours it like Michelin star cuisine. Could this be my million-pound idea runs through his head as he places the empty pot on his bedside table. Rab pulls the duvet over and crashes out.

Another morning arrives; as always, there are consequences from the previous evening. A burning smell comes from the pot at the side of the bed. It has stuck to the table and has to be struck hard to break the bond created as it burned itself onto the tabletop last night, having been put there while still hot. There are strange, coloured stains on the pillows and sheets. These appear to be spillage from the grotesque mix of beans and coco pops. Shaking his head as he tidies up, Rab tries to accept every day with whatever surprises may greet him. It's just part of life now.

There is a feeling of success swirling around Rab as he finishes tidying up. He thinks, 'is the juice worth the squeeze?' and concludes that it is. If this is as bad as it's gonna get when I'm puffing strong weed, then my plan has been a success, and it's the way to go. The big benefit from last night was no drink or coke, just the weed and some silly munchies. 'I've cracked it this time. Bring on the weekend.'

Friday arrives...

'Alright, Joe. It's young Rab. What ye up tae later? I'll tell ye why I'm askin. I've got a new plan tae smoke weed and chill in the hoose, watch a movie, or get the tunes oan. I'm still gonna have a few bevvies, but my plan is tae stay away from the coke as I'm sick of all the fuckin carnage it brings.'

'Aye, OK, Rab. That sounds alright tae me—a wee night in yer hoose wi a bevvy an a bit of puff. Will I get a few bodies organised and we'll turn it intae a wee party? Asks Joe.

'Aye, why not. You organise a few bodies and we'll huv a good laugh. Mind, I'm no wantin tae get involved wi any snortin,' says Rab.

'Leave it with me, and I'll see ye later.' Replies Joe as he hangs up the phone.

Joe arrives later with eight other party participants, three of whom Rab has never met. The bevvy is flowing, and the tunes are oan as the wee party starts gathering pace. Some more bodies are phoned, and before Rab knows what's happening, there's about twenty people in his hoose. Rab is enjoying himself as he gets progressively more wasted. The bevvy, combined with the weed he's smoking, is hitting the spot, and he's determined not to participate in the consumption of cocaine.

Young Rab has always used cocaine when he's oan the bevvy, and its use has enabled him to drink a lot more than he should be able to handle. Tonight, it seems, he has forgotten that as he gets caught up in the party atmosphere and throws back the bevvy like a thirsty man in the desert. Without the coke to help him stabilise and deal with copious amounts of bevvy, he gets very drunk very quickly. It's lights out early for Rab...

Another morning/afternoon arrives as he awakens on his couch with horrendous memory loss and troubling flashbacks. Rab surveys his house in dismay. The place is a fuckin riot. There are empty bottles everywhere, and some had spilled over. His good rug is soaking and stained. His house looks like it's been broken into and trashed. Here we fuckin go again, thinks Rab as he surveys the carnage.

He goes to the kitchen and luckily finds an unopened bottle of beer which he decides is the very thing to help steady his nervous disposition. Opening the cupboard where he keeps his monthly rent money adds to his problems. His rent money has gone. Six hundred pounds he had put aside has gone, and Rab is ready to burst into tears. He makes his way to the toilet shaking his tormented head, wondering what the fuck his life has become. Rab looks in the mirror to discover that his front tooth is missing...

'No more parties for me.'

As hard as he tries to keep his act together when he's sober, the next binge is never far away. (Rab is on the binge merry-go-round of having to tidy up and clean up after every expedition. His new plan of smoking lots of weed doesn't seem to be working).

After a couple of hours, things are looking better. The place is looking a lot tidier, and on we go. Three bin bags are taken outside, full of empty cans and all sorts of waste. Rab decides his rug will have to go as it's stinking and stained. As he rolls it up, his day gets a little brighter because the missing tooth is hiding under the rug. 'Ya dancer, I'll glue that back and be looking handsome again in no time.' He gets a wee flashback of a tussle with someone at the party and a punch getting thrown. Rab feels a wee bit cringe'y but dismisses it as he is beyond caring.

This week turns out to be quite productive as Rab goes to work and involves himself in some healthy eating. Overall, things are pretty good. In fairness, when Rab is straight and away from temptation, he is a good worker and well-liked. He is in a fortunate situation with work that he can turn up whenever possible, partly because his boss is an understanding, decent person who empathises with what Rab is going through and wants to be supportive. For how much longer, that's anybody's guess. A successful week is had, and Rab feels good. He stuck the tooth back with Gorilla glue, and it's been rock solid all week. Friday arrives, and wages are paid. 'Will I see you on Monday, Rab?' his boss asks. 'I hope so, John, I really do. I'm gonna try stay out of bother this weekend...'

The phone goes.

'Rab. It's Joe. Whit ye uptae? That wiz some party last weekend, man. What a nick we were in. Ye comin doon the pub man, it's Friday ffs.'

'Listen, Joe. I'm tryna take it easy man. A canny cope wi gettin gaga every fuckin weekend.'

'Rab, c'mon doon the pub. It's Friday, man; ye know ye want tae. Ma cousins are up for the weekend, and ye always get a laugh wi them.'

Rab arrives at the pub, and we're away again...

Rab, Joe, and Joe's cousins.

Joe's three cousins have arrived for the weekend, and boy, do they like to party. His three cousins are female, and one of them has brought her boyfriend, a man of moderation, a more sensible type. The drink starts to flow, and everyone is getting into the party mood. Rab nips outside wi Joe for a joint in the hope that it helps keep him away from the coke.

As the drinking gathers pace, the offer of a party comes up. Joe persuades everyone this party sounds like a good idea, and they jump in taxis and get to the address.

Another fuckin party thinks Rab, fuck it; I'm here noo.

As they find a spot to plank themselves down, the party's host comes over and gives Rab a small packet containing some E's. 'Mitsubishi,' exclaims Rab. 'Who's up fur a couple of E's.'

They all take two each, apart from the sensible boyfriend one of Joe's cousins brought along. Rab can't understand what she's doing with someone sensible like that, but he accepts there are many things in life he can't understand.

On with the party.

The conversation is flowing as the E's are kicking in. A few folks are dancing, and the party is revving up. Rab is getting on well with one of Joe's cousins, one for whom he's always had a wee thing. She's laughing at his jokes, and there have been no uncomfortable silences. Things are going good, and Rab thinks he may have a chance of some romance here.

The E's are strong, and Rab feels it surging through his body. He's feeling mighty fine. She says something to Rab that he finds funny, and suddenly he's laughing almost uncontrollably, an unusual kind of laugh, a kind of laugh/snort, snort/laugh. What the fuck kind of noise is coming from me?'

Just at that moment, Rab snort/laughs, and his tooth leaves his open mouth like an Exocet missile. The Gorilla glue has given up. He glances at the tooth travelling at supersonic speed as it hits the eyeball of his love interest. She lets out an almighty scream and throws her hands up to cover her face.

Oh no, thinks Rab, as commotion breaks out.

To be continued...

You, yes you. Do you feel a bit confused? How do you think Rab feels?

What happens to young Rab?

Does he continue sliding down the slippery slope into the darkness?

What will the next fuck up be?

Will he decide enough is enough and seek help?

We will catch up with him again, real soon.

Suppose you know anyone struggling with addiction, addictive behaviours, or mental health issues. Be supportive, be there for them. Be kind.

When you can't look on the bright side, I will sit with you in the dark.

Alice in Wonderland.

If you've managed to get this far, then I salute you, but before you go. The final story is an idea for a Novella. It's an old-school murder/whodunnit-type story. Let me know what you think.

A Novella?
'A Strange Wee Toon' (working title).

It's early morning and misty. A dog walker is on his usual route; all is well, and the dog is enjoying his daily adventure. The dog runs off the path and disappears into the bushes—nothing unusual in this, as the dog likes to explore. Then the barking begins, and the owner calls for his dog to return. After repeated calls, the owner enters the bushes to find the distraction holding his dog's attention.

A dead body.

This body is a gruesome sight. The body is barefoot, and the left arm is missing. The face is unrecognisable and beaten to a pulp. All this is too much for the dog walker, who vomits and screams for help.

(The discovery of the arm takes place later during the search, and it's found in a wooded area about half a mile away)

That's how it all starts.

Two local Detectives are given the responsibility of piecing together what has happened. These two Detectives are well-known in the area, having worked this patch for many years. Overall, they have many successes and are considered reasonably competent.

Not so much success in recent times, though!

Detectives Forest and Newton have been in partnership for a long time. Outside appearances give the flavour of two colleagues having become friends over years of bonding through various experiences as policemen. This couldn't be further from the truth. Detective Forest intensely dislikes Newton and mostly wishes all sorts of badness upon him but keeps this quiet and plays the part of his friend (They had a close friendship for many a year, but since 'the incident,' things changed between them).

Detective Newton has only two years of service remaining before he can collect his pension and sail off into the sunset. He was a good policeman in his day, but now, he is a liability. Newton is barely able to hang onto his job. He drinks too much and, more recently, has become incompetent.

Despite the unpleasant feelings, Detective Forest always looks out for Detective Newton. Other officers wonder why Forest goes right out of his way to cover for Newton, as sometimes, it seems, he puts himself at risk trying to keep Newton in the clear when he fucks things up. The real reason is Newton knows a dark secret about Forest (the incident), which would finish his career and make his life miserable if it were to surface.

So, we have this underlying tension between the two detectives as they try to find the killer. This dark secret, or 'the incident' as it is known between them, will slowly reveal itself as the case unfolds.

Now, back to the murder victim.

The body turns out to be someone involved in the local drug trade. As the case unfolds, an associate of the victim, someone regarded as a person of interest, is also found dead after being given a large amount of drugs and left unconscious on his living room floor. His house is then set on fire, where he is found lifeless. Let's call him Callum.

Why was he silenced? What's his connection to the first murder victim?

Criminologist and profiler 'Dougie' is brought in to help with the case. Dougie is the big brain. His profiling skills are known throughout the country. His reputation precedes him. He knows Forest and Newton from his youth as they grew up together in the area and share the same local pub.

One of the main suspects turns out to be a local boy called Drew H, a known supplier of various drugs. Drew H moves substantial quantities and has been on the police radar for quite some time. His drug empire covers an area with a radius of about ten miles. Is murder something that Drew H is capable of?

Drew H likes to dabble with drugs, although he is tee-total with regard to alcohol. His choice of drug is LSD acid, and he likes to get fucked up with his hallucinogenic delights. Mental health-wise, he is borderline something. No one knows what he is, just that he is borderline something and not playing with a full deck. Drew H lives in a beautiful, expensive flat in the village, which most locals assume was acquired with drug money.

(The flat was part of an inheritance left for Drew H, but this is not known locally) This flat is always immaculate, and I mean pristine. The reason for this, as the detectives will find out when they attempt to question him as a suspect, is because Drew H lives in one of the cupboards within the flat. He doesn't use or touch any other part of the flat out with the cupboard that he lives in.

His head is fried from years of acid use, and he has developed some strange beliefs. Although he is a fruit-loop, this doesn't seem to have affected his ability to deal drugs and the cash incentives it brings him.

The above description of Drew H gives a flavour of the type of people our second victim, Callum, hung around with and a possible connection to the first murder victim, the one-armed corpse.

As the case unfolds, it turns out that Callum was holding themed parties. He was a bit mental and also bisexual. Callum liked people to dress up, which was why his parties were themed. No dressy upsay, no getting in. He would have sixties-themed nights, period drama-themed nights, gay nights, and futuristic-themed nights. These wild party nights at Callum's are connected with the dark secret Detective Newton has about Detective Forest.

We follow Detectives Forest and Newton as they try to gather evidence and leads in their pursuit of justice and attempt to find the murderer or murderers.

Along this journey, there will be introductions to

other people of interest as the case builds and the Detectives possibly, close in on an arrest.

We will get to know the Detectives better and learn more about their character as they pursue the killer or killers. Callum has an interesting role as his connection with the first victim, his association with Drew H, and his relationship with the Detectives are revealed.

Who murdered the one-armed corpse?

Who drugged and set fire to Callum's house, killing him?

What's the dark secret (the incident) Detective Newton has about Detective Forest?

Will there be an arrest?

Try not to let all the good stuff go to your head, nor take the bad stuff to heart. It's just life.

Finally

Shout out, and thanks for the feedback. You know who you are.

Wait, wait, there's a bonus story from my friend. I hope you enjoy it...

CHRISTMAS SPIRIT

by
Alan McGeachie

Christmas is coming, and I always enjoy the anticipation of it. I like the slightly 'supernaturalesque' element to the festive season, a bit like Dickens; A Christmas Carol; dark but ultimately with a message of hope and love that transcends time.

I had an experience once, not frightening, but it seemed to be part of that year's Christmas plan.

As a retired Police Officer, I often think about it as the festive season approaches. Picture the scene; I'm walking a busy city centre street on my beat, resplendent in my uniform, bulled boots like mirrors, creases in my trousers and tunic like blades, the peak of my cap pulled over my nose like a guardsman, the epitome of professionalism.

As I passed the Buchanan hotel, a regular haunt for the residue of humanity that would pour out its doors hourly, my radio crackled to life. 'Could an officer attend the Buchanan hotel regarding a potential missing person'? Well, I was outside it and wasn't up to much anyway, so I diligently responded and told the static-voiced controller that I was a short distance away and would attend. My short distance away amounted to about three feet.

I got the story from the manager, who didn't look much older than me and seemed to care about most of his wayward guests.

The manager told me It was a young lad home from the Merchant Navy. He had a lot of money in his pocket, but with a secret, he did not want his family to know. The shame kept him away so much that he was shacked up in a shabby city centre hotel, lonely and despondent.

Nineteen years old with a drinking problem! That's what two years in the Merchant Navy travelling the world can do to a young, immature lad, I was told.

After a few days of searching, I found him in a pub just south of the river, drowning his teenage sorrows. He was in a real state, drunk, emotional, and unhappy with life. I called his home, which was up north, and spoke to his mother and let her know where her boy was. I informed her in my best officious tone, which melted away to that of a concerned parent (I had recently become a proud Father and was keen to show my empathic side). She said someone would be at that pub in two hours. "Guaranteed," she said keenly. True to form and believing that I had won her over (parent to parent), I gave her my mobile number just in case she wanted to call me for updates. The boy's mother was very agreeable to this and repeated my phone number vigorously, and I could tell she was jotting it down.

Two hours passed to the minute when a man walked into the pub, approached the bar, and ordered a half and a hauf (a half pint of beer and a whisky). (I maybe should have explained that in my efforts to trace the lad, I had reverted to plainclothes to conceal my Identity as bar staff are now reluctant to serve Police officers in full uniform alcohol in full view of the public!) The man slowly turned his head left and right to inspect the inside of the pub and have a good look at its patrons, nothing unusual for a first-timer in a new hostelry.

I will never forget the look on the man's face as his gaze flitted from my face to the face of my young drunk charge. "Davie!" he exclaimed in bewildered surprise and nearly leaped the ten-foot distance towards us in one step. "Da, is that you?" The Father grabbed his Son and drew him to his feet; both hugged each other as they had never hugged before.

Davie buried his head in his Father's shoulder and sobbed uncontrollably. I could tell the Father was trying to hold on to his emotions in front of the strangers surrounding him.

"Thank you for coming so soon; that was very helpful," I said, proud of my efforts reuniting the family, Father, and Son. I'm glad your Wife got the message to you so quickly I exclaimed with a grin on my face that I could not help.

"Eh, whit!!" the father said. I could see the ridges on

his forehead starting to peak like roughly ploughed furrows' as his thick black and grey eyebrows began to meet, the boy stopped crying and looked at me blankly.

The Father spoke again, "What are you talking about, Son? I'm just off the boats; we're heading back out in two hours. I'm just having a fly pint."

My grin had dropped to a perplexed, confused stare, and I knew I had gone quite red. Confusion was clouding my thoughts. "Why......why.... what made you come in here? I asked in a searching, confused tone.

"I don't know," even he sounded surprised, "Wouldn't normally come this way, usually stay close to the docks, just fancied a walk, but I couldn't walk past this place, don't know why. Ah, don't even like these types of pubs, too poncy."

"But what about the call from your Wife? she said you would be here in two hours. 'Guaranteed,' she said. She was very adamant," I explained.

"Ma boat docked two hours ago, Son, and here I am."

And then he said it. I will never forget what he said next, "Ma Wife died two years ago just after the boy went to sea."

Ice ran down my back like a waterfall, and I could feel the hairs on my arms stand up as firm as hundred-year-old oak trees.

"It broke her heart to see the boy go. I think that's what finished her."

My mind was whirling so much I could feel myself getting weak. I decided I had better leave. I wished Father and Son the very best for the festive season and every good fortune for their new-found futures together. We all shook hands vigorously before I half ran, staggered to the door, and went out into a cold crisp neon-lit Christmas night and home.

Two days later, it was Christmas Eve. I, my Wife, and our new baby were just about to head out and join the great family Christmas Eve gathering made all the more special by all our latest additions on both sides of the family. Just as I was about the turn the lock on the front door, my mobile phone started to buzz in my pocket, 'Come on!' I thought annoyingly, 'Who phones at this time on Christmas Eve.' Unless it was my brother instructing me to get more beer. I pulled the phone out of my pocket and looked at the screen. My annoyance was compounded by the fact that I did not know the number or even recognise it.

I pressed the green answer button and, in a rather aggravated tone, stated, "Hello," as business-like as I could muster.

"Is that Constable McGeachie? I found your name and number on a pad next to my phone in the hall."
"Funny, it's my wife's writing,"

There was a pause in our conversation that I will never forget, not uncomfortable, but the realisation that something had taken place that neither of us could explain or understand. " My Son and I decided not to go back to sea as he's going to get help with his drinking and enter rehab. I'm giving him all my support, and we will build bridges and be a family. I love my boy and want him to be healthy and happy again. Merry Christmas, and thank you." the Father said.

"No, no, thank you," I said meekly as I got into the car. I knew then the Father, and I had been part players in a celestial conspiracy to save a boy from the edge of the abyss. Deep down, I felt humbled to have been chosen to play my part. "Linda Ronstadt," the Father said, jolting me back to the present, "Sorry," I answered in a somewhat perplexed tone that even surprised my Wife!

"'Somewhere Out There, It's playing on your radio; that was my Wife's favourite song; it gave her hope, she always said."

There was nothing to add. I closed the phone and put it back in my pocket. I listened to the words of the song playing, and at that very moment, it all made sense.

The disbelievers can disbelieve; the mickey takers can take the mick, but I knew then what it all meant, and I felt the most relaxed and contented I had ever felt.

My Wife drove that night as I mulled over the last three days of a very strange but very special Christmas that will always be part of the fabric of my own special Christmas season.

'Somewhere Out There,' mmh, it's a thought, isn't it?

About the Author

Walter Scott lives on the outskirts of Glasgow in a small place called Milngavie (known locally as Mulguy). 'I used to wrestle a bit and then have a few pints, or maybe I used to have a few pints then wrestle, I can't remember. Living the quiet life now.

Printed in Great Britain
by Amazon